SECRETS OF MANGA AND COMIC BOOKS

Eddie Robson

CLASH

by ticktock

Copyright © ticktock Entertainment Ltd 2008

First published in Great Britain in 2008 by ticktock Media Ltd,
2 Orchard Business Centre, North Farm Road, Tunbridge Wells, Kent, TN2 3XF

project editor and picture researcher: Ruth Owen
ticktock project designer: Sara Greasley

With thanks to series editors Honor Head and Jean Coppendale,
and Joe Harris

Thank you to Lorraine Petersen and the members of nasen

ISBN 978 1 84696 748 1 pbk

Printed in China

Picture credits (t=top; b=bottom; c=centre; l=left; r=right):
2000 AD & Judge Dredd © & ® Rebellion: 16t, 16b. Antiques & Collectables/Alamy: 14, 15. Asian Art & Archaeology,
Inc./Corbis: 20. Dave Bartruff/CORBIS: 1. Julia Bax and Eddie Robson: 26, 27t, 27b, 28. Adek Berry/AFP/Getty Images:
4b. Bettmann/Corbis: 11. Mike Blake/Reuters/Corbis: 29. Vince Bucci/Getty Images. Spider-Man™ & © 2008 Marvel:
13. 3 x 3 Eyes copyright © 1990 by Yuzo Takada. All rights reserved. Originally published in Japan in 1990 by Kodansha
Ltd., Tokyo. Appleseed Hypernotes copyright © 1996 Shirow Masamune. All rights reserved. Originally published in
1996 by Seishinsha. Club 9 copyright © 1993 by Makoto Kobayashi. All rights reserved. Originally published in Japan in
1993 by Kodansha Ltd., Tokyo. Seraphic Feather copyright © 1997 by Hiroyuki Utatane and Toshiya Takeda. All rights
reserved. Originally published in Japan in 1997 by Kodansha Ltd., Tokyo. Shadow Star copyright © 2000 by Mohiro
Kitoh. All rights reserved. Originally pubished in Japan in 2000 by Kodansha Ltd., Tokyo. What's Michael? copyright ©
1995 by Makoto Kobayashi. All rights reserved. Originally published in Japan in 1995 by Kodansha Ltd., Tokyo: 24.
Richard Felton Outcault, Buster Brown (July 7, 1907) Prints and Photographs Division, Art Wood Collection, Library of
Congress: 8t. FocusJapan/Alamy: 22-23. goldenagecomics.co.uk: 9. HULK. ™ & © 2008 Marvel Entertainment, Inc.
Used with permission: 12. Images © the DFC (artist John Aggs; writer Philip Pullman): 17t, 17b. Manjunath
Kiran/epa/Corbis: 4t. Iain Masterton/Alamy: 25b. Istock: OFCtl, OFCbr. Nocella/Three Lions/Getty Images: 10.
PALESTINE © Joe Sacco; art reproduced with the permission of Fantagraphics Books: 19t. Jupiter Images: 21. Karl
Schoendorfer/Rex Features: 2. Shutterstock: OFCtc (x2), OFCtr, OFCc, OFCcl, OFCcr, OFCbl. Sony Pictures/Everett
Collection/Rex Features. ™ & © 2008 Marvel. © 2007 Columbia Pictures: 6-7. Sony Pictures/Everett Collection/Rex
Features: 18. Doug Steley B/Alamy: 31. Amet Jean Pierre/Corbis Sygma: 25t. The Lone Wolf & Cub © 1995 KOIKE
KAZUO & KOJIMA GOSEKI. All rights reserved. First Published in Japan in 1995 by KOIKE SHOIN PUBLISHING CO.,
LTD., TOKYO. English translation rights arranged with KOIKE SHOIN PUBLISHING CO., LTD: 23. 2002 United Feature
Syndicate, Inc. Reproduced by permission: 8b. John Van Hasselt/Corbis: 5. Warner Bros./Everett Collection/Rex
Features: 19b.

Contents

CHAPTER 1 A WORLD OF COMICS

Comic books have been around for about 75 years. Today, they are created and enjoyed all over the world. People of all ages read comic books.

A comic book artist at work in Bangalore, India.

A young Indonesian boy reads *The 99*. This comic book features 99 superheroes. They are the world's first Islamic superhero team.

A young Tibetan man enjoys a comic book about the Belgian character, Tintin.

5

Spider-Man 3
movie 2007

Comic books have given the world superheroes such as Spider-Man and Superman.

Spider-Man is one of Marvel Comic's most popular superheroes. Peter Parker became Spider-Man when he was bitten by a radioactive spider –

- Spider-Man can stick to any surface
- He can lift 10 tons
- His spider sense warns him of danger

Comic books have also been the inspiration for blockbuster movies!

CHAPTER 2

THE EARLY DAYS

Comic strips first appeared in the late 1890s in American newspapers. In 1895, the comic strip *Hogan's Alley* began using the speech bubbles we still see in comic books today.

The Yellow Kid

Hogan's Alley featured a group of children living in a poor area of New York City.

One of the children, the Yellow Kid, became a huge hit with readers.

Newspaper comic strips are still popular today. Many have been running for years.

Peanuts in Spanish

Peanuts first appeared in a newspaper in 1950. Today, it is still read by 350 million people, in 2,500 newspapers, in 75 different countries!

In 1934, Eastern Colour Press published *Famous Funnies.* It was an 8-page book that re-used newspaper comic strips.

Soon, American publishers were producing comic books with new material. They also created new characters who appeared from one week to the next.

CHAPTER 3 AMERICAN COMIC BOOKS

In 1938, two comic book fans, Joseph Shuster and Jerry Siegel sold some comic strips they had created to American publisher DC Comics.

The strips were about a character with superhuman powers – Superman!

Superman appeared in issue one of DC's *Action Comics*. The superhero comic book was born and...

...readers loved it

Comic books about characters, such as Wonder Woman, Batman and The Flash soon followed.

After a few years, crime and horror comic books became the top-selling titles in America.

Then, in the 1950s, a campaign started in America to ban these comic books.

Some people said comic books would turn young readers into thieves, bullies and killers!

Some schools even held comic book burnings.

A publisher shows artwork that has been changed to fit new comic book rules.

In the end, comic book publishers set up their own strict set of rules.

Artwork was changed. Words such as "terror" and "horror" could not appear on covers.

In the 1960s, comic book fans were introduced to the Fantastic Four, the Incredible Hulk, the X-Men, Iron Man and Spider-Man.

These famous characters were created by writer Stan Lee for Marvel Comics. Lee worked with artists such as Jack Kirby, Don Heck and Steve Ditko.

Jack Kirby's *Incredible Hulk* cover artwork

Marvel's heroes didn't just fight bad guys. They also had real-life problems, such as girlfriend and school troubles.

"I wanted the hero, Peter Parker, to be a teenager, and my publisher said, a teenager can't be the hero... teenagers can just be sidekicks."

Stan Lee

Writer Stan Lee

CHAPTER 4

BRITISH COMIC BOOKS

British comics, such as *The Beano* and *The Dandy*, have usually been aimed at very young readers.

The Beano and *The Dandy* were first published by Scottish publisher D.C. Thomson in 1938.

Issue from 1957

Issue from 1957

Early issues of *The Beano* and *The Dandy* are very rare. This is because readers were asked to recycle their comics to save paper during World War II.

In the late 1970s and early 1980s, British comic books such as *Warrior* and *2000 AD* were published.

These hard-hitting, yet humorous comic books were aimed at teenagers.

2000 AD introduced Judge Dredd – judge, jury and executioner in an American city of the future.

2000 AD first issue 1977

2000 AD cover featuring Judge Dredd 1978

One of the writers on *Warrior* and *2000 AD* was British writer Alan Moore.

Moore also wrote the award-winning *Watchmen*. It tells the story of a group of past and present superheroes. Many comic book fans think *Watchmen* is the best comic book ever.

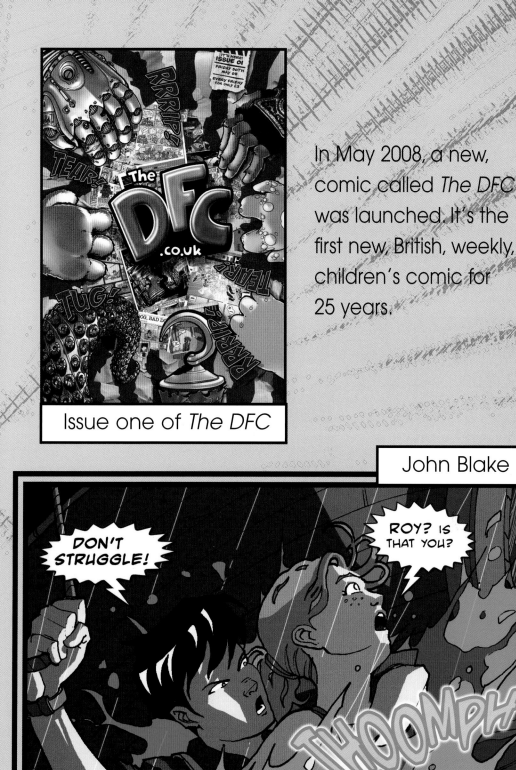

In May 2008, a new, comic called *The DFC* was launched. It's the first new, British, weekly, children's comic for 25 years.

Issue one of *The DFC*

John Blake

DON'T STRUGGLE!

ROY? IS THAT YOU?

THOOMPH

The DFC features "John Blake", a story written by bestselling author Philip Pullman.

CHAPTER 5 GRAPHIC NOVELS

In the late 1970s, comic book creator Will Eisner wrote and drew the first graphic novel – *A Contract with God*.

Other artists and writers began to create graphic novels for older readers and adults.

Today, graphic novels are available in most bookshops, on many different subjects.

French-Iranian artist and writer Marjane Satrapi created the graphic novel *Persepolis*.

It tells the story of her childhood in Iran during difficult political times.

Artwork from the animated movie of *Persepolis* from 2007.

Joe Sacco is a journalist. His graphic novels present facts about situations around the world.

Sacco's graphic novel *Palestine* looks at the lives of Palestinian people living with poverty and war.

Palestine 2001

The movie *300* released in 2007

Many graphic novels have been made into movies. The movie *300* is based on Frank Miller's graphic novel about a battle in ancient Greece.

CHAPTER 6 MANGA

Japan had been producing stories with pictures for hundred of years. Then, in the 1940s, Japan discovered comic books!

An adult picture story from 1885.

After World War II, American soldiers were stationed in Japan.

When the Japanese saw the soldiers' American comic books, they quickly started to make their own comic books, known as manga.

Manga can be hundreds of pages long.

Now, around two billion manga comic books are sold each year in Japan.

People of all ages read manga. They are cheap to buy and cover subjects from sci-fi to basketball!

Readers can even enjoy manga in 24-hour cafes. They pay a small hourly fee to read from up to 30,000 books.

Osamu Tezuka is known as the "God of Manga".

Tezuka started writing and drawing comics in 1946, when he was still a teenager.

The wide-eyed style of some Japanese manga characters was invented by Tezuka. He got the idea from Disney cartoons.

Tezuka died in 1989. He left behind more than 700 volumes of manga. That's over 150,000 pages on many different subjects.

**Tezuka took some ideas from the movies.
He would often put together panels without words.**

"Silent panels" give a fast, dramatic flow to the action.
It's just like watching a movie.

Sometimes a manga with over 300 pages can be read in just 20 minutes.

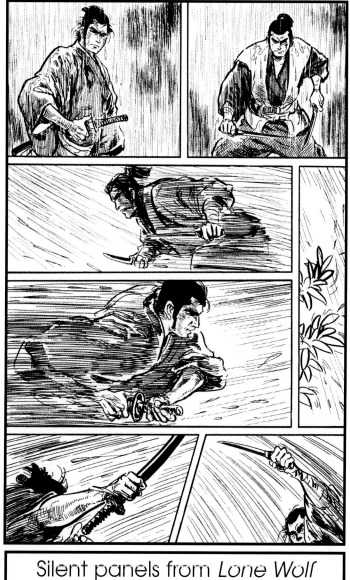

Silent panels from *Lone Wolf and Cub* by Kazuo Koike and Goseki Kojima.

At first, manga was not well known in Europe and North America. However, in the 1980s, Japanese cartoons called "anime" came to this part of the world.

Anime have the same look as manga, and most artists create material for both.

Anime became popular and an interest in manga started to grow. By the 1990s, more and more manga was being translated into English.

The *Dragon Ball* manga was translated after the worldwide success of the anime version.

It takes a lot of work to translate manga.

Japanese sentences usually read down rather than from left to right.

Japanese books are also read from the back to the front.

CHAPTER 7 CREATING COMICS

The main jobs in the creation of a comic are:

- Writing
- Pencilling
- Inking
- Colouring
- Lettering

These jobs can all be done by one person,
or by different people.

First, the comic is written as a script by the writer.
The writer writes the captions and speech.
The writer also describes what happens in
each panel for the artist.

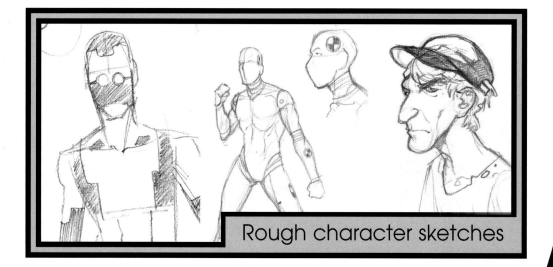

Rough character sketches

Next, the script is passed to the penciller.
The penciller is the main artist on a comic.

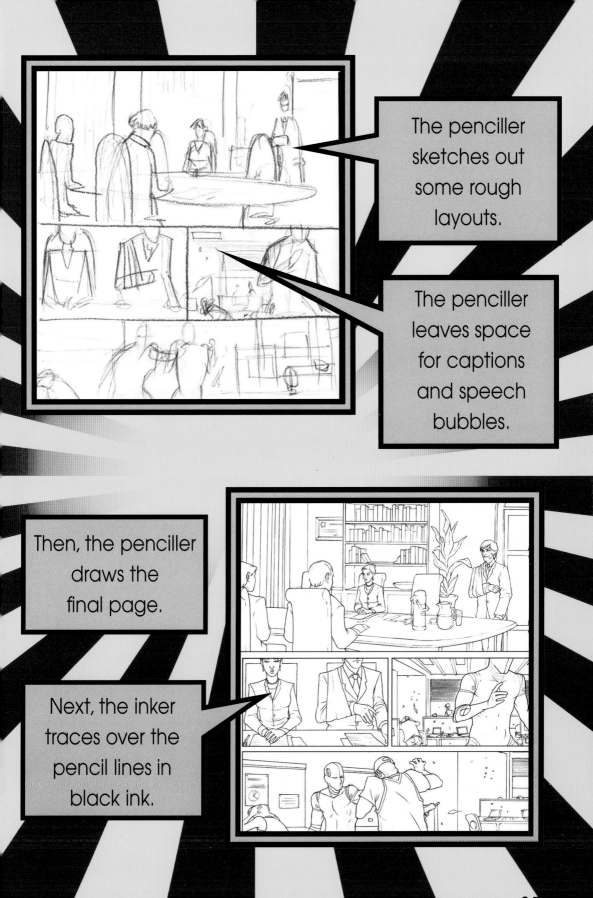

The penciller sketches out some rough layouts.

The penciller leaves space for captions and speech bubbles.

Then, the penciller draws the final page.

Next, the inker traces over the pencil lines in black ink.

Next, the colourist adds in the colours.

The finished page

Finally, the letterer writes all the words into the caption boxes and speech bubbles.

Many comic book readers want to write or draw their own comic books.

If they can't find a publisher, they often print and sell their own comic books. This is called self-publishing.

Comic book conventions are a good place for self-publishers to sell their books.

Fans with their goodies at a convention.

Self-published manga are called "dojinshi".

At manga conventions in Japan, big publishers look for the mangaka (artists) of the future.

NEED TO KNOW WORDS

anime The Japanese word for animation. It's actually the same as the English word – it's just been shortened.

campaign When a group of people take actions to try to make something happen.

comic book A book or magazine which contains stories told in pictures and words.

comic book convention A meeting where comic book fans can buy and sell comics. Creators can talk about their work, and show their new ideas.

executioner An official who puts someone to death.

graphic novel A long comic book that is created to be published as a book.

inspiration The idea behind something.

Islamic A person who is a Muslim and follows the faith of Islam.

judge A person who decides if someone is or isn't guilty of a crime, and says what their punishment should be.

jury A group of people in a court who decide if a person is or isn't guilty.

manga The Japanese word for comics.

publisher A company that creates and sells comic books, magazines, newspapers or books.

radioactive Something that gives off harmful radiation.

rare Not many of something.

script A document which contains all the text which will appear in a comic book. A script for a play or movie contains all the speech and instructions for the actors.

translate To change something from one language to another.

MORE FACTS FOR THE FANS

- Most comic book fans collect comic books. Rare comic books can be very expensive. The first issue of *Action Comics* which features Superman is one of the world's most rare comic books. A copy in good condition is worth over £235,000.

- Japan's "Super Comic City" convention has over 18,000 stalls selling self-published dojinshi. In the USA, most comic convention visitors are male. At "Super Comic City", about 90% of the visitors are female.

- The internet is now an affordable way for comic book creators to make their work available. They simply put it on a website!

Fans at manga conventions often dress up as their favourite character.

COMICS AND MANGA ONLINE

Websites

http://www.comicbookresources.com

http://www.newsarama.com

http://en.tezuka.co.jp/

http://www.howtodrawmanga.com

INDEX